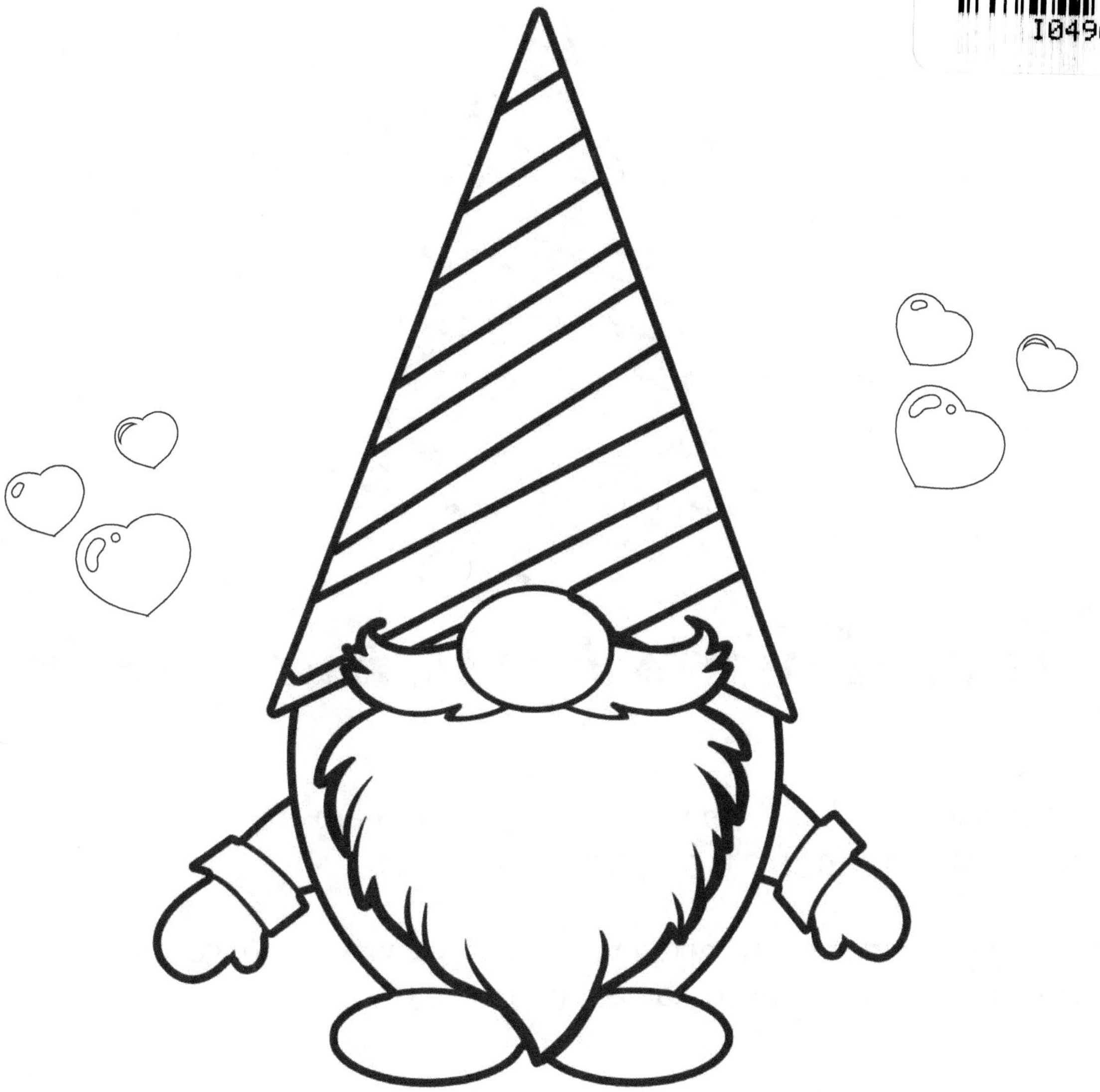

WITH MY

whole heart

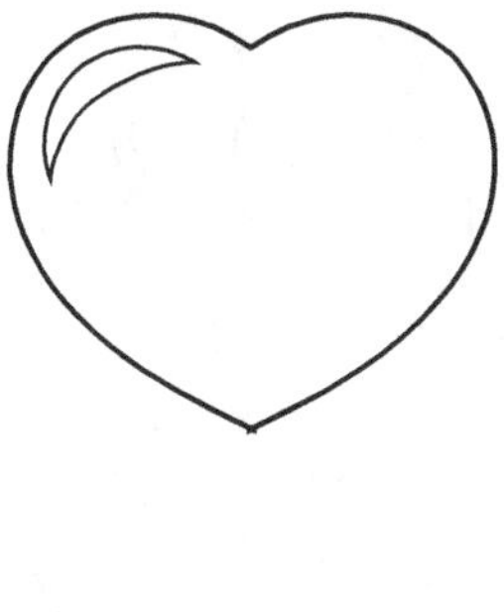

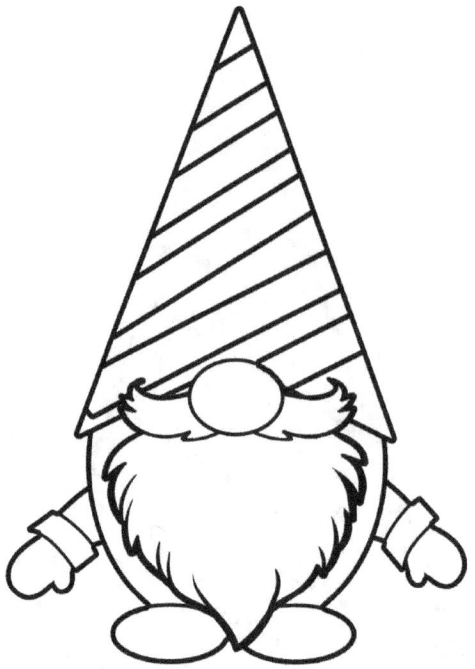

Tips and hints for using this book

- This paper works best with pencils, keep them sharp and use layers of color rather than pressing really hard the first time

- Use pencils or test other mediums on the two back test pages to check for bleed through or try out color combinations

- Write about romance or gratitude or color selection on the lined page behind each coloring page or leave blank if there is bleed through

- Put a piece of paper or light card behind the page you are coloring on so you don't make indents on the next page

- Done is better than worrying about perfection, don't stress over colors or mistakes

- Start anywhere – at the front, in the middle, the last one

- This is a book designed to be used by YOU, so please add more lines, backgrounds, washi tape etc., if you are feeling creative.

Copyright @ChattyFred 2020

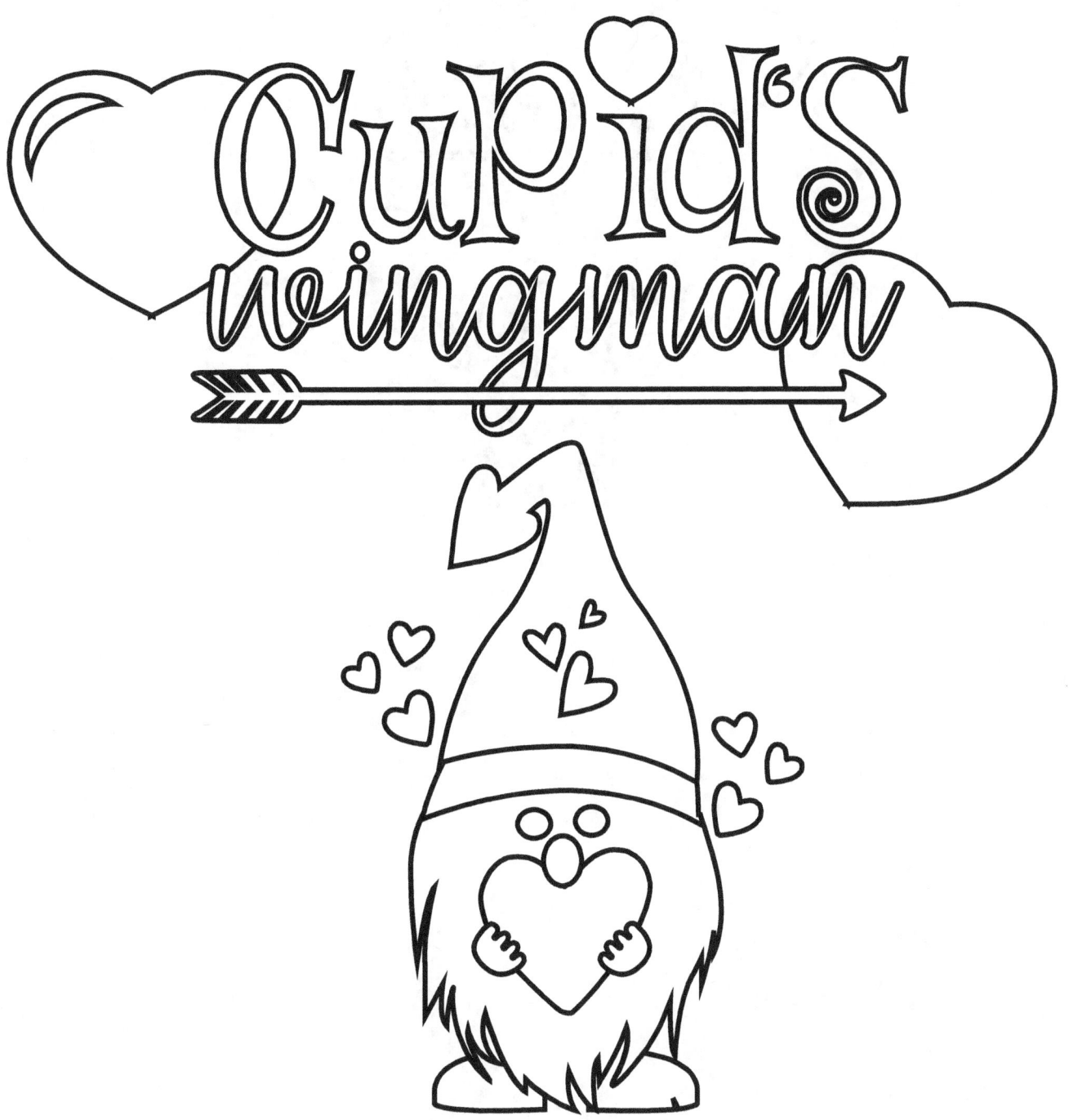

Colored by:	
Date completed:	
Pencils/mediums used:	

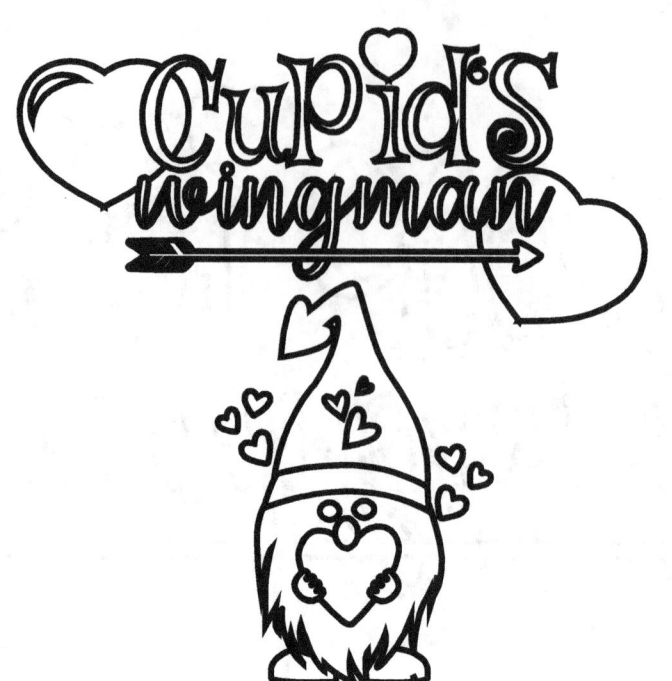

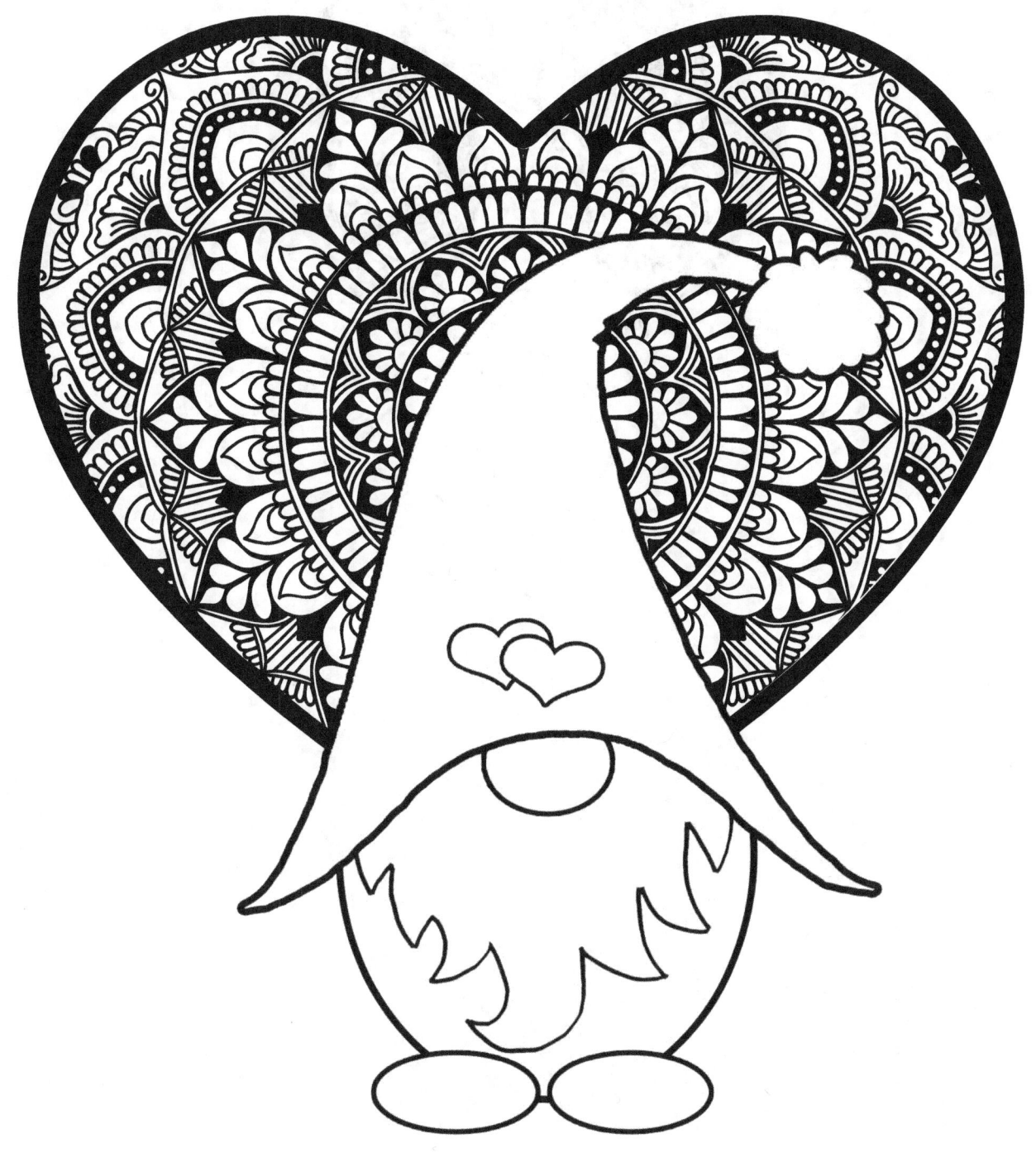

Colored by:	
Date completed:	
Pencils/mediums used:	

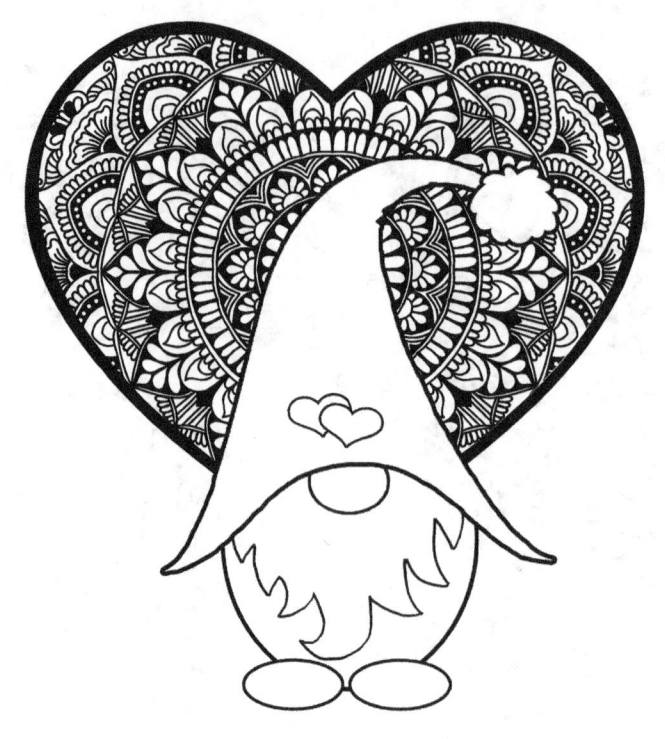

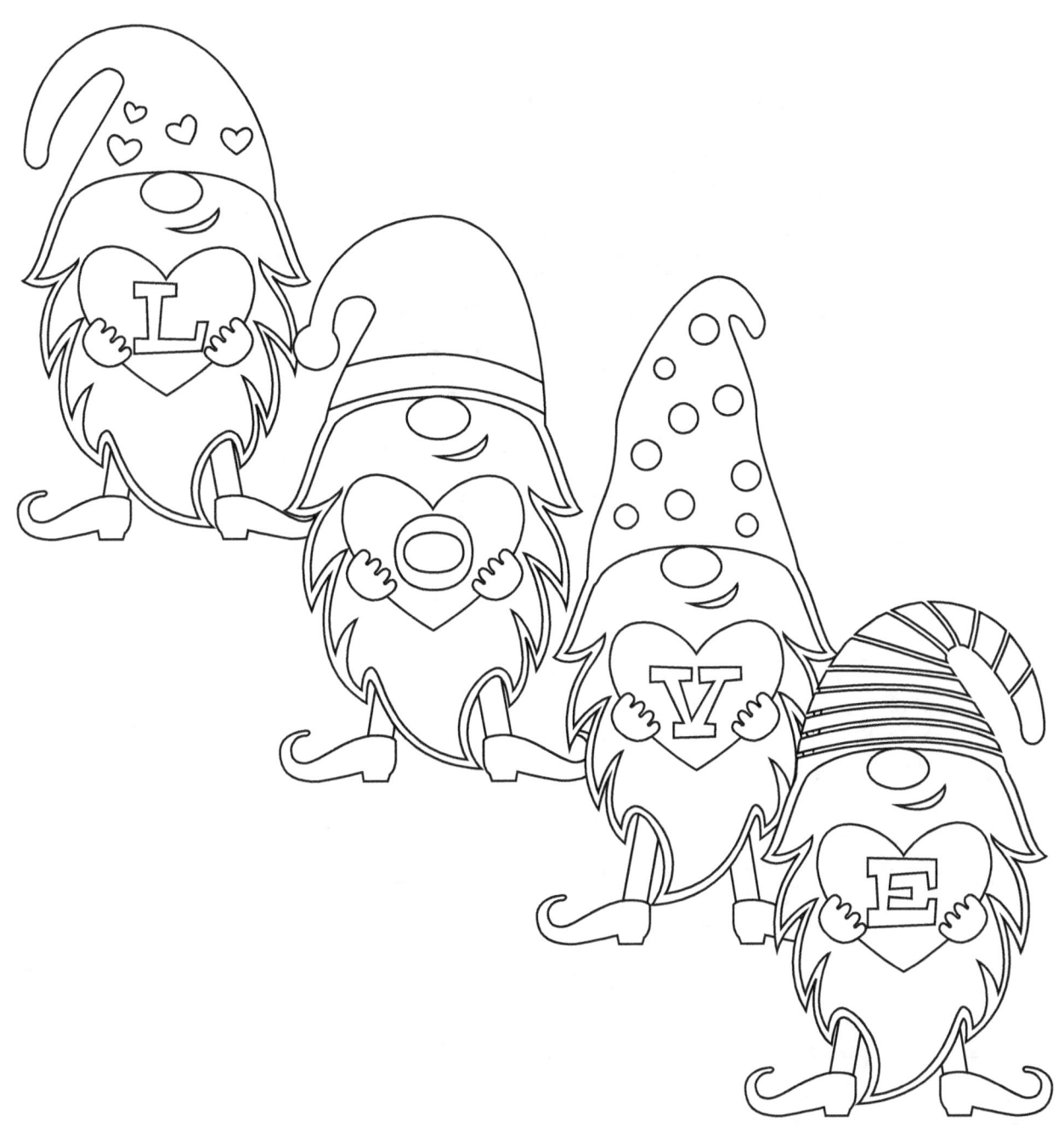

Colored by:	
Date completed:	
Pencils/mediums used:	

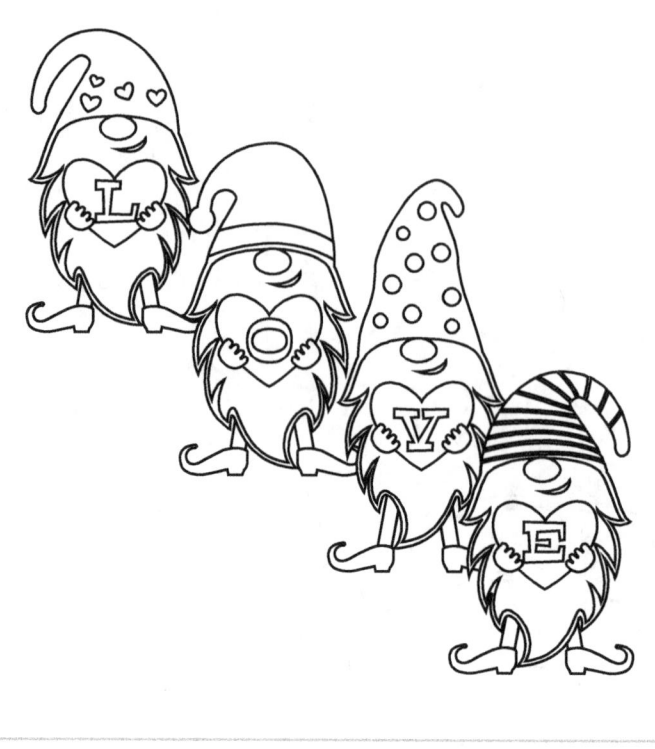

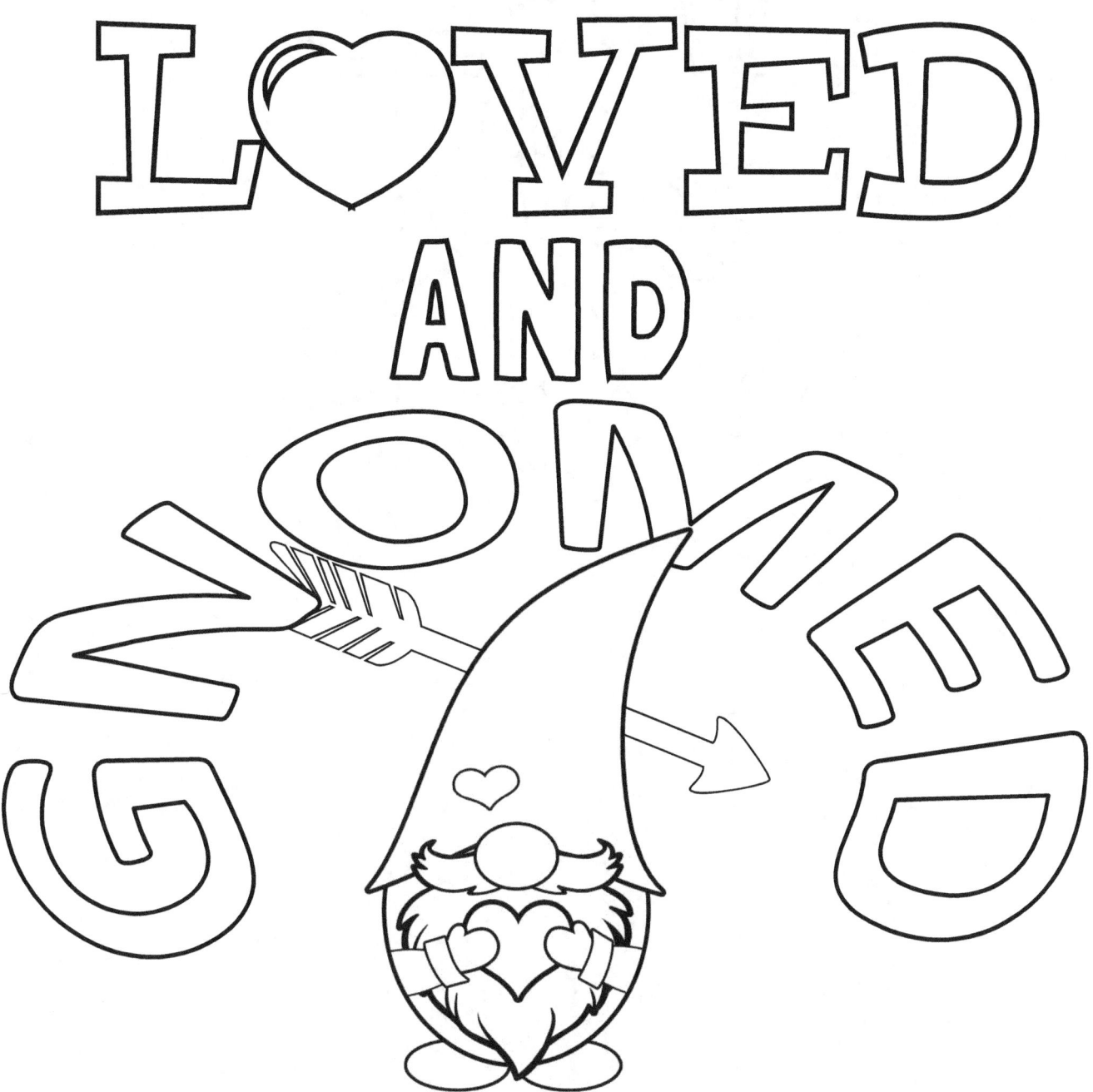

Colored by:	
Date completed:	
Pencils/mediums used:	

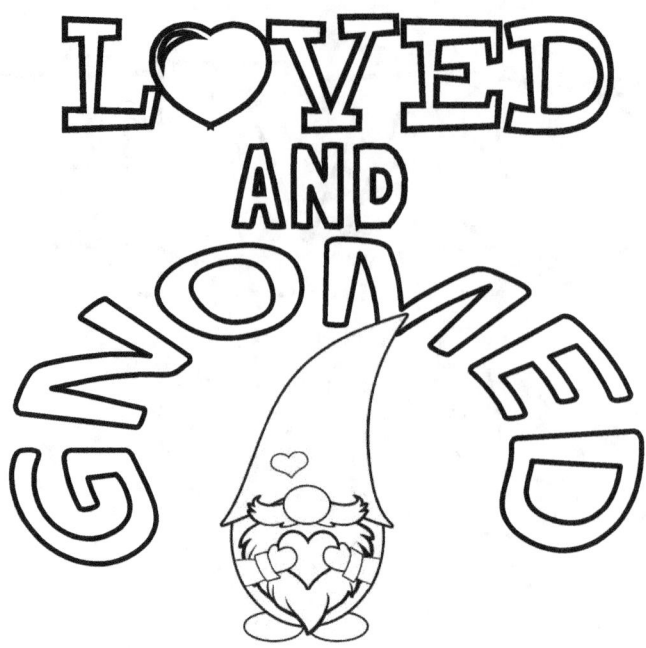

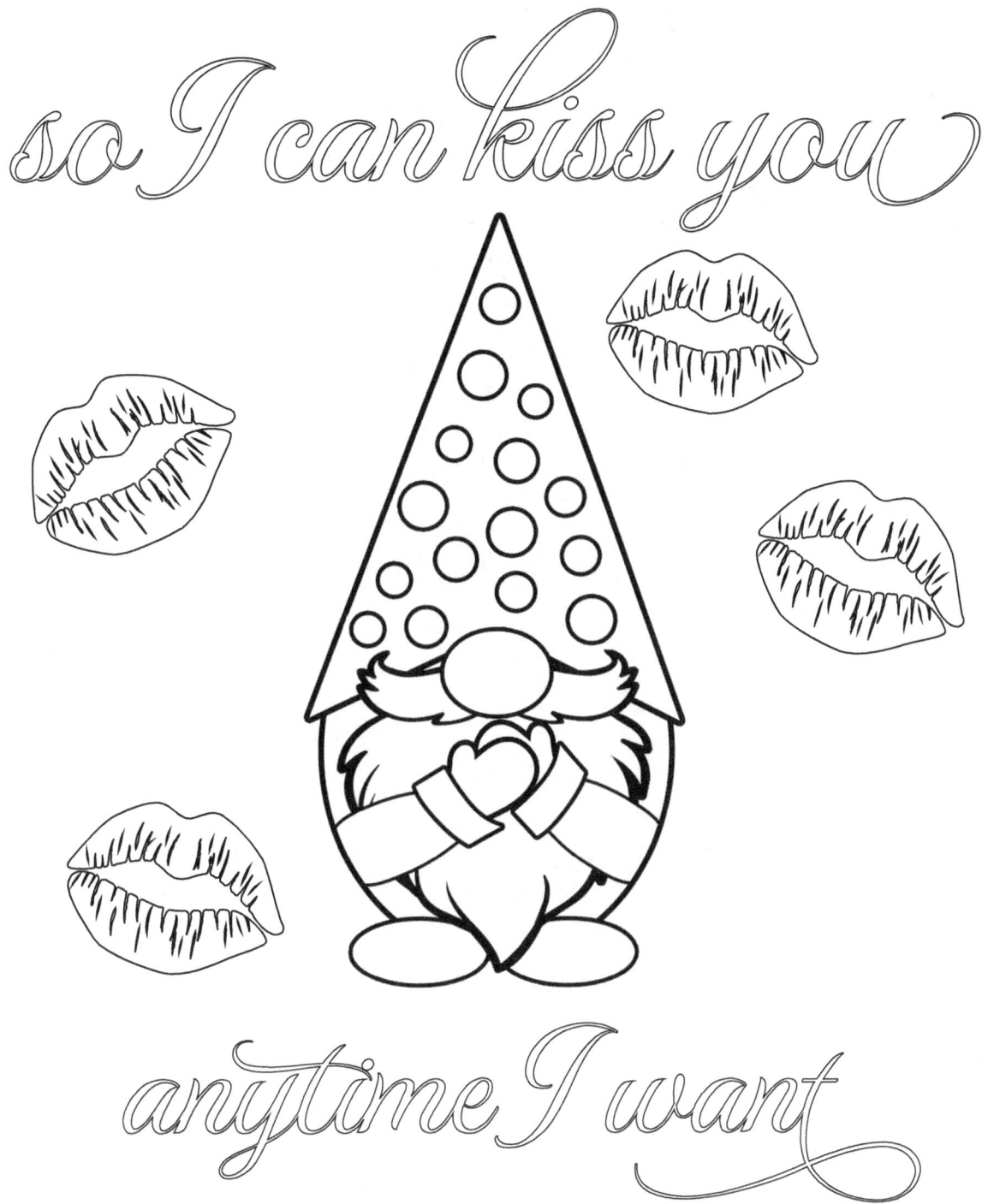

Colored by:	
Date completed:	
Pencils/mediums used:	

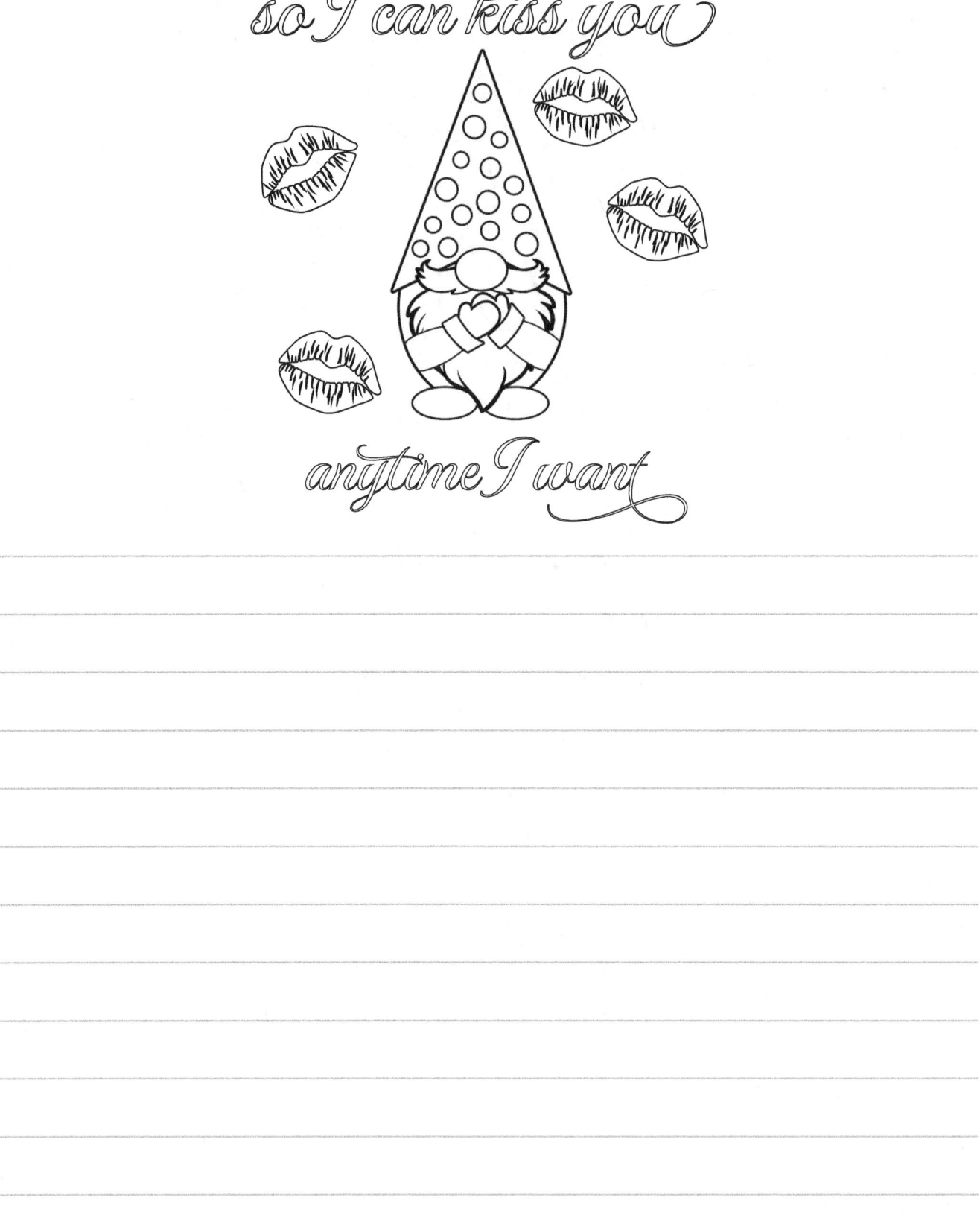

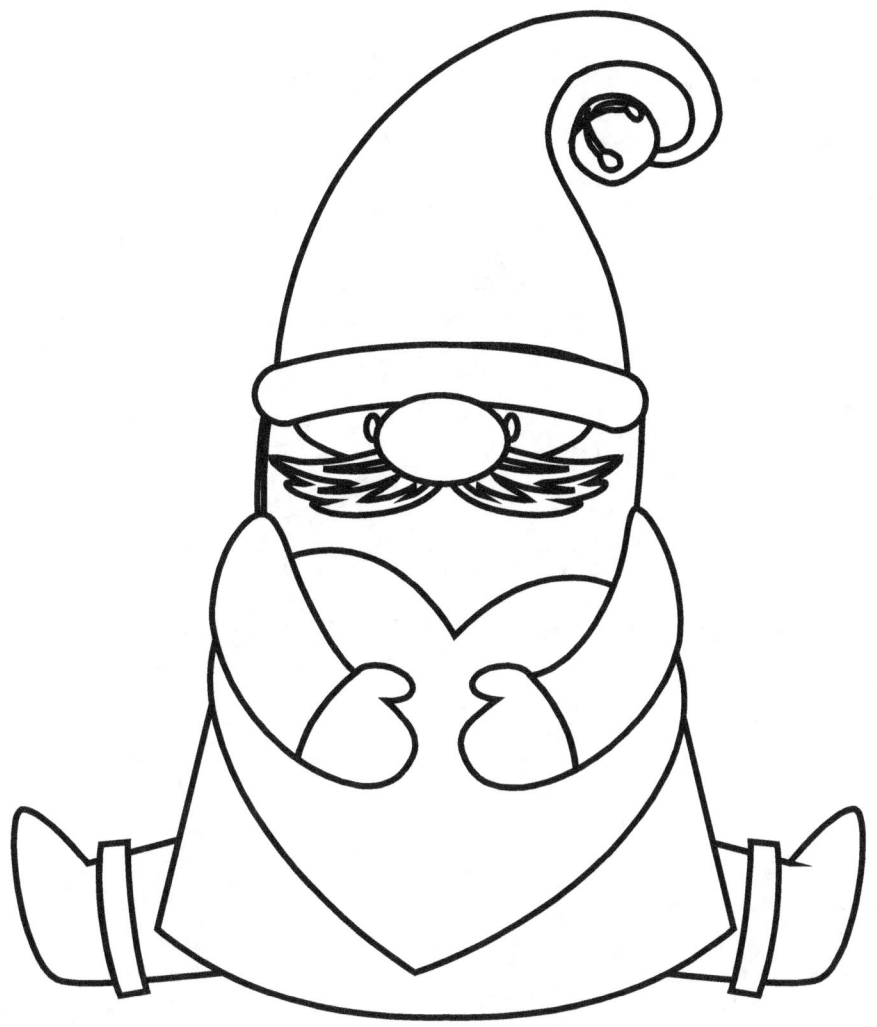

MAY MY HEART BE YOUR SHELTER
and my arms be your home

Colored by:	
Date completed:	
Pencils/mediums used:	

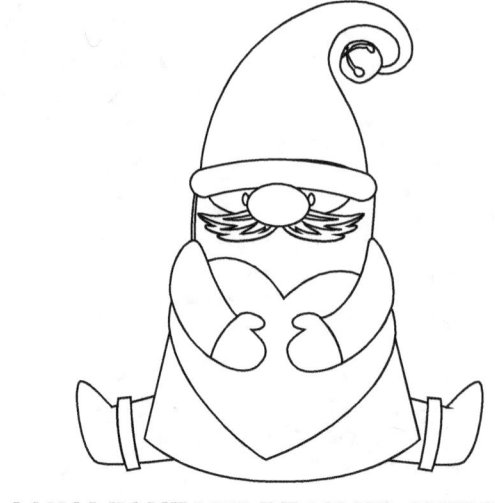

MAY MY HEART BE YOUR SHELTER
and my arms be your home

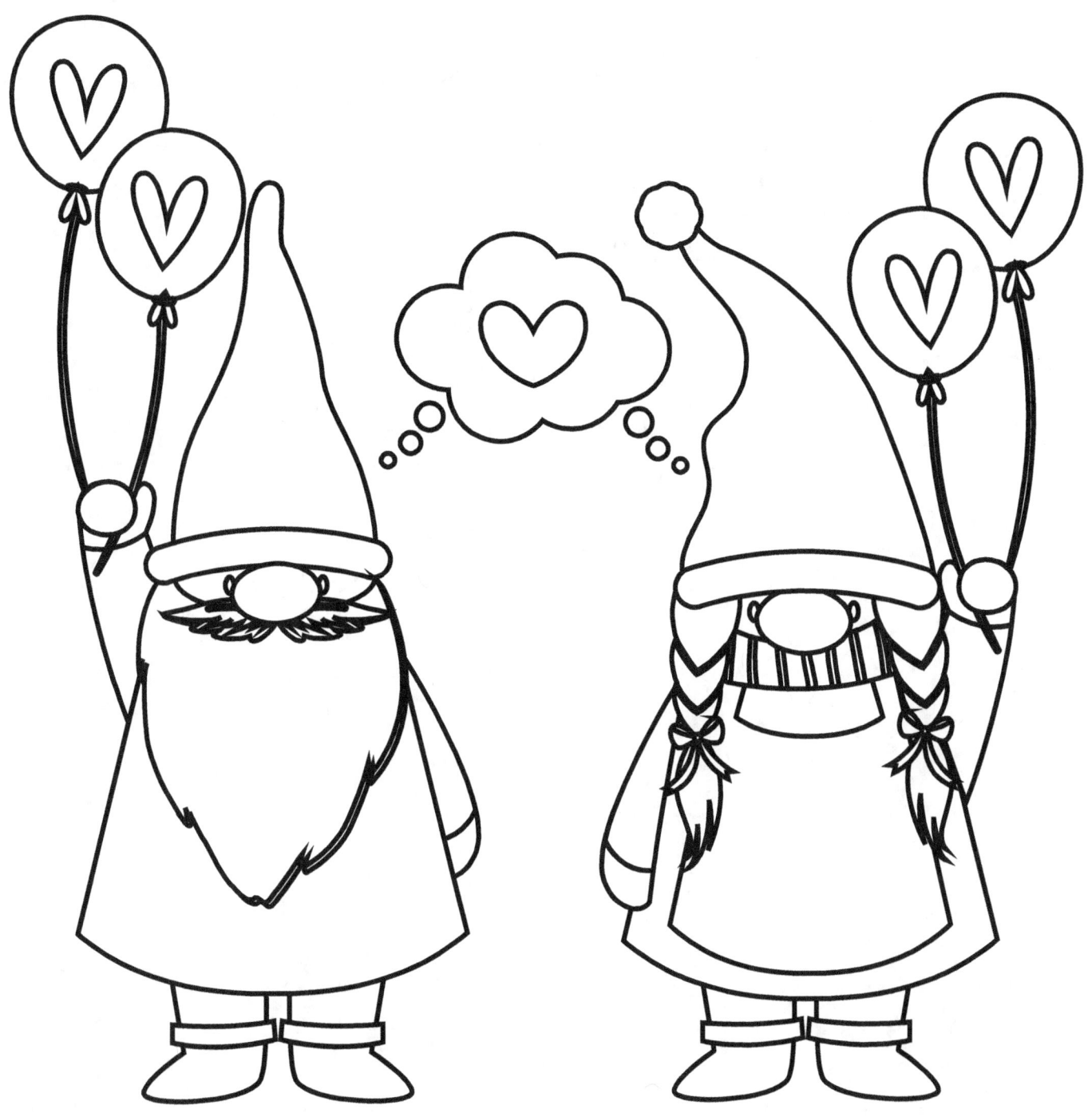

Colored by:	
Date completed:	
Pencils/mediums used:	

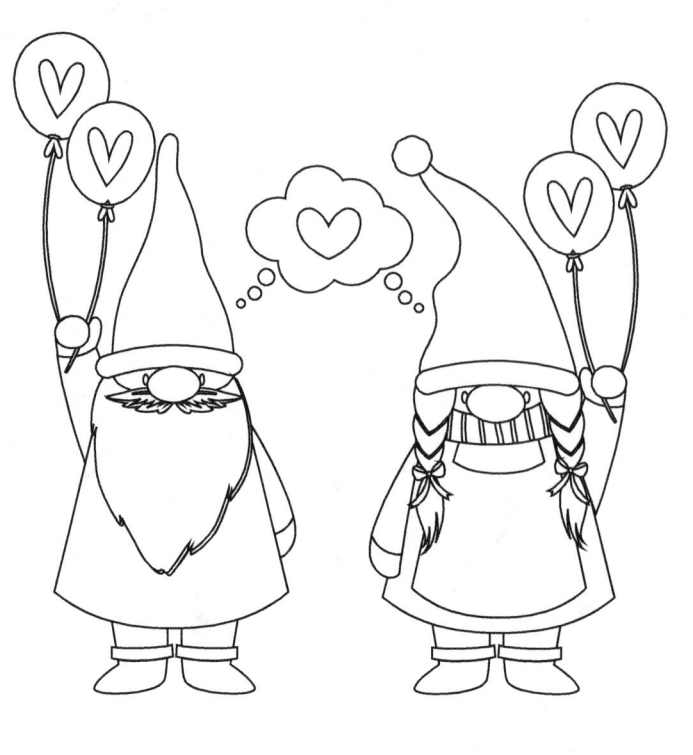

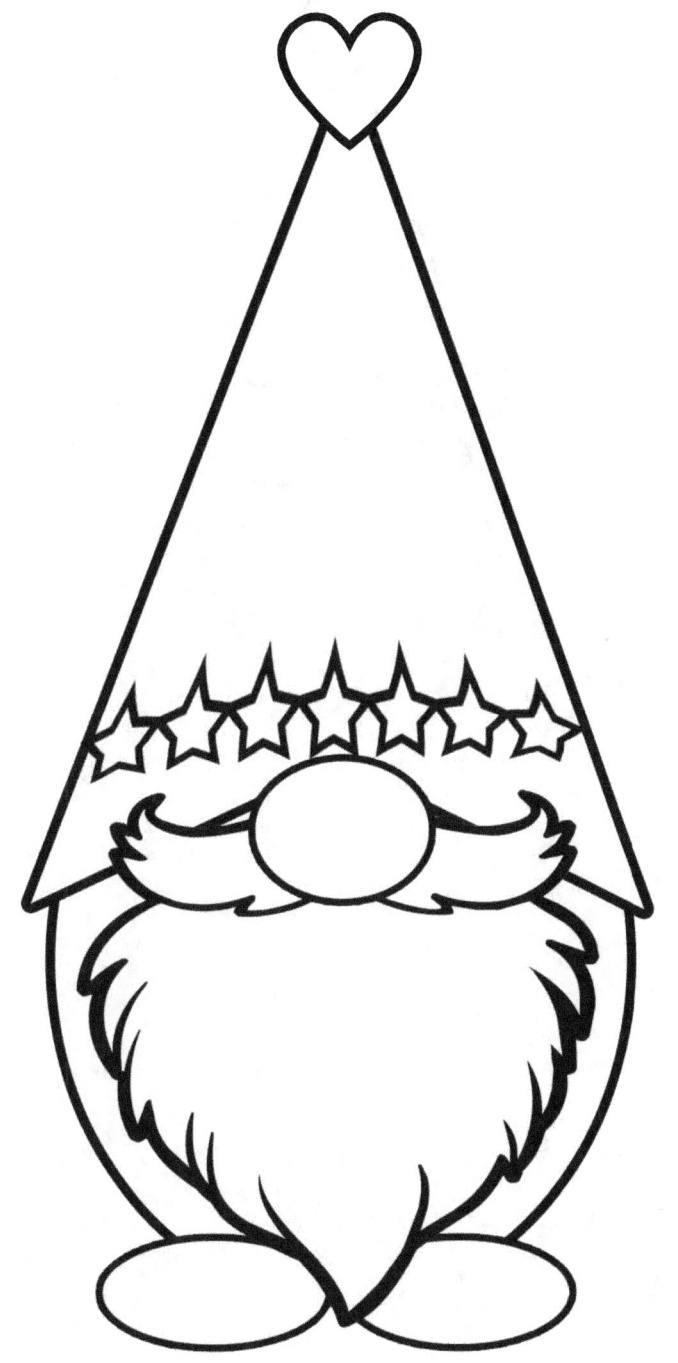

Colored by:	
Date completed:	
Pencils/mediums used:	

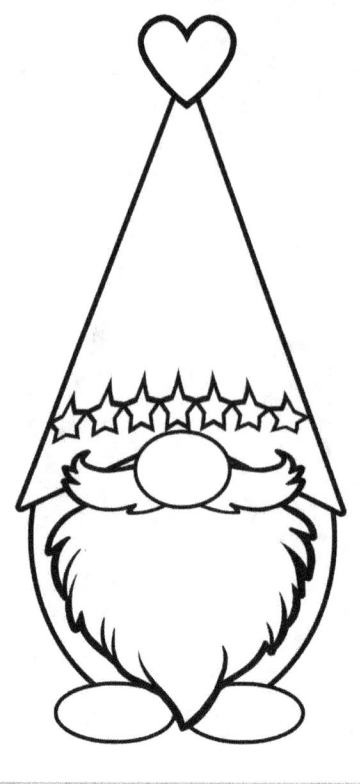

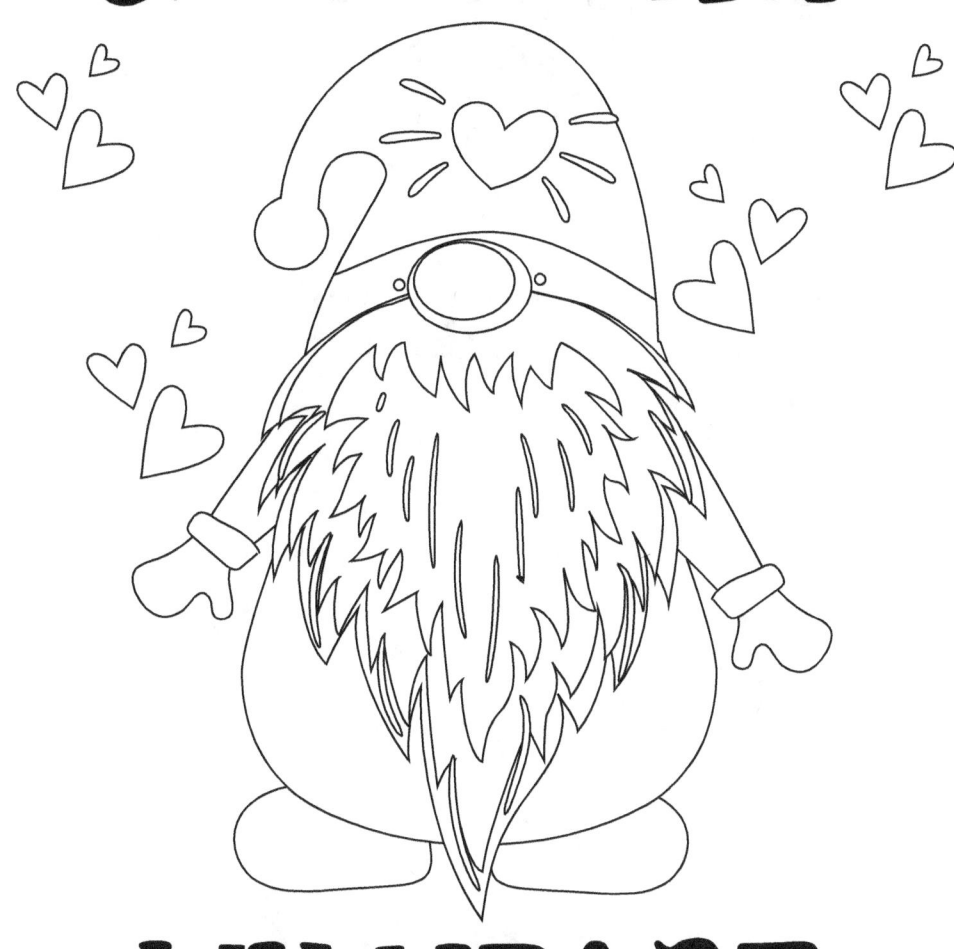

Colored by:	
Date completed:	
Pencils/mediums used:	

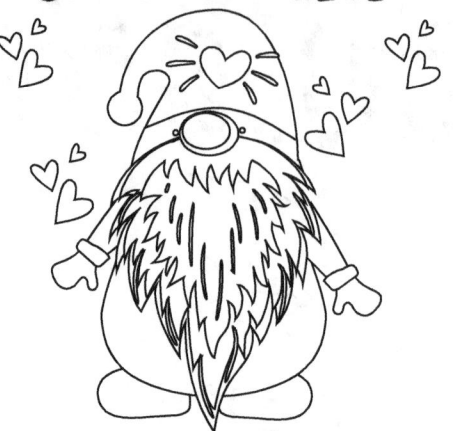

YOU GOTTA MY HEART

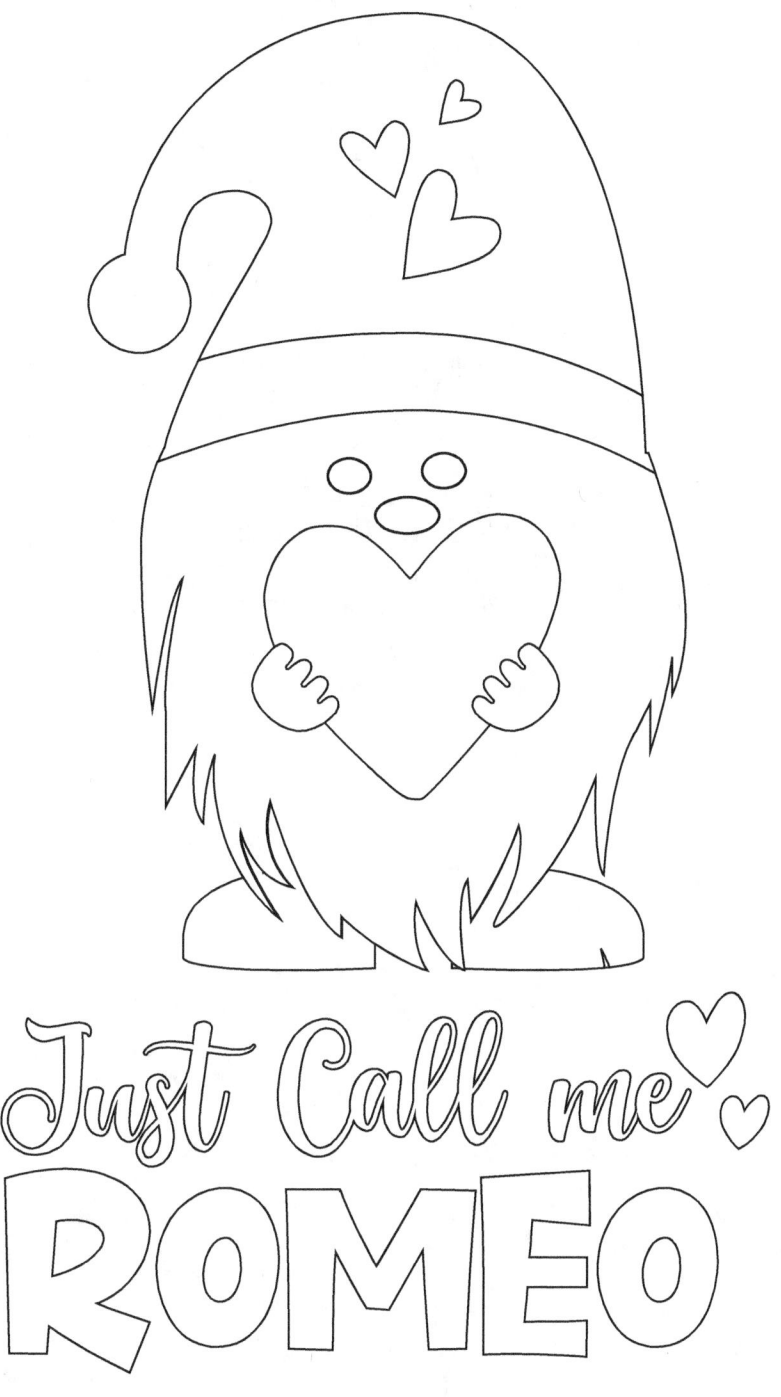

Colored by:	
Date completed:	
Pencils/mediums used:	

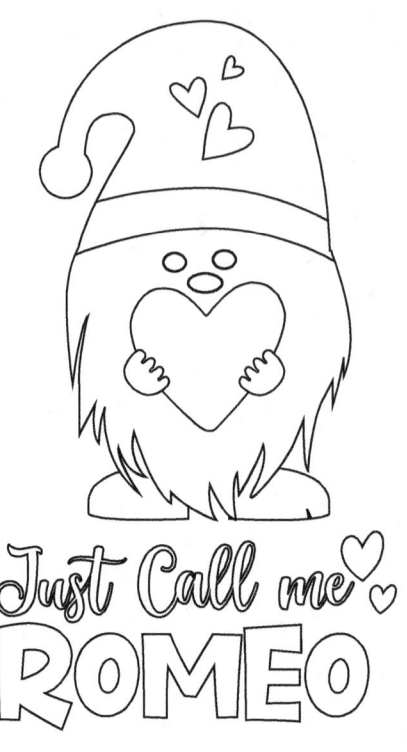

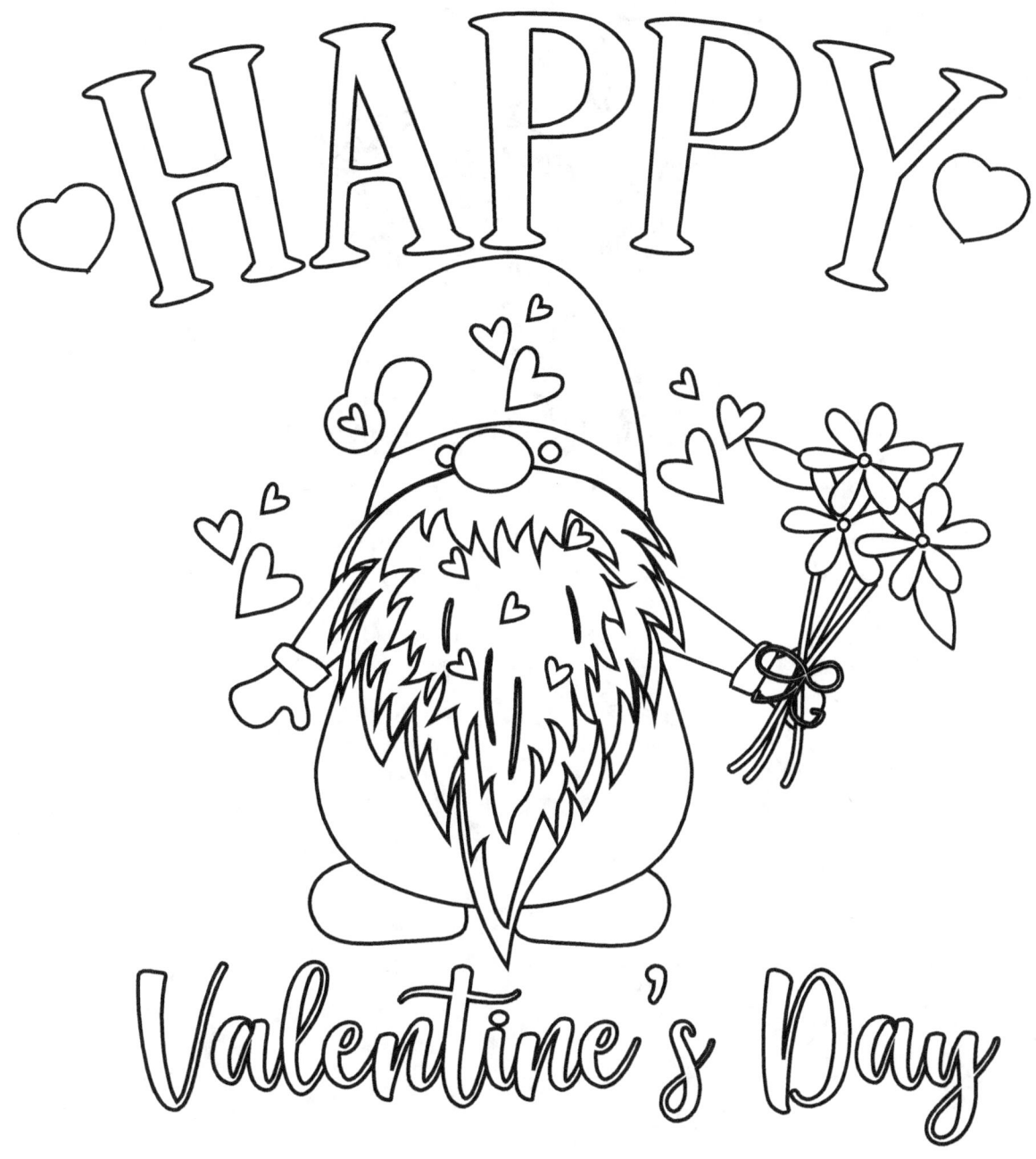

Colored by:	
Date completed:	
Pencils/mediums used:	

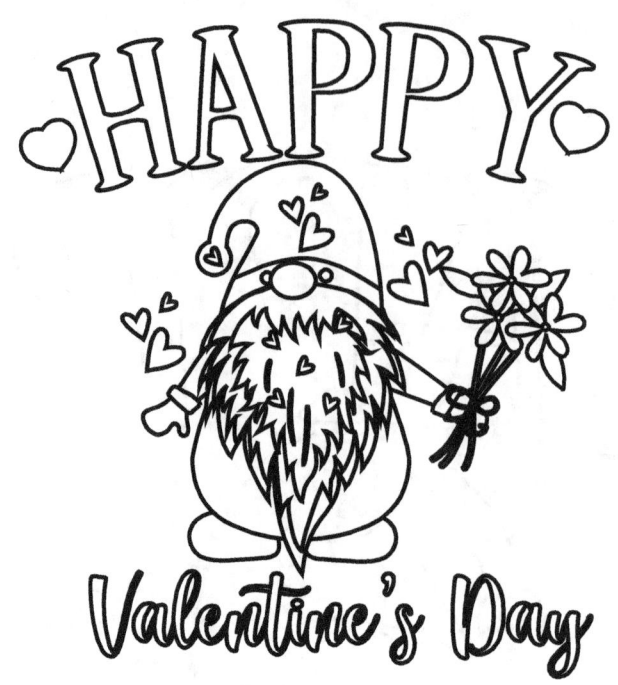

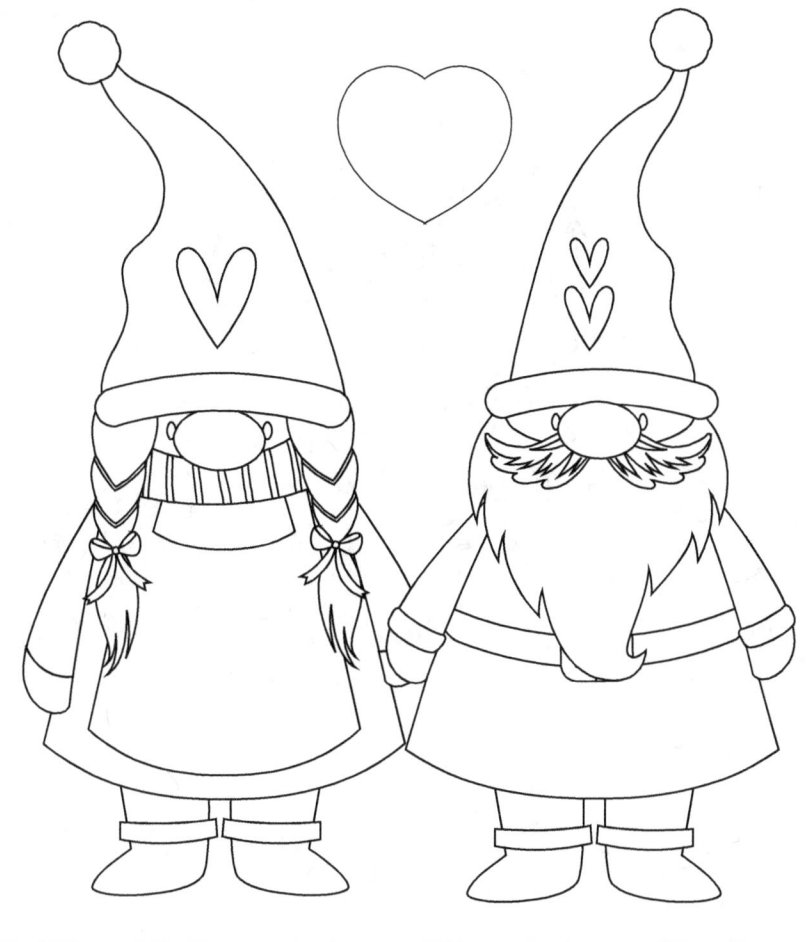

THIS IS US
our life our story our home

Colored by:	
Date completed:	
Pencils/mediums used:	

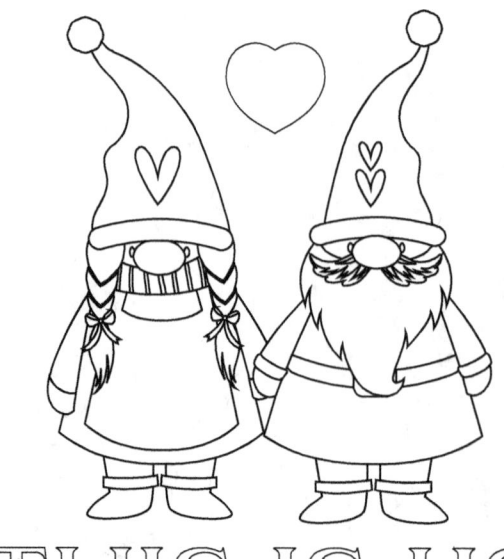

THIS IS US
our life our story our home

Colored by:	
Date completed:	
Pencils/mediums used:	

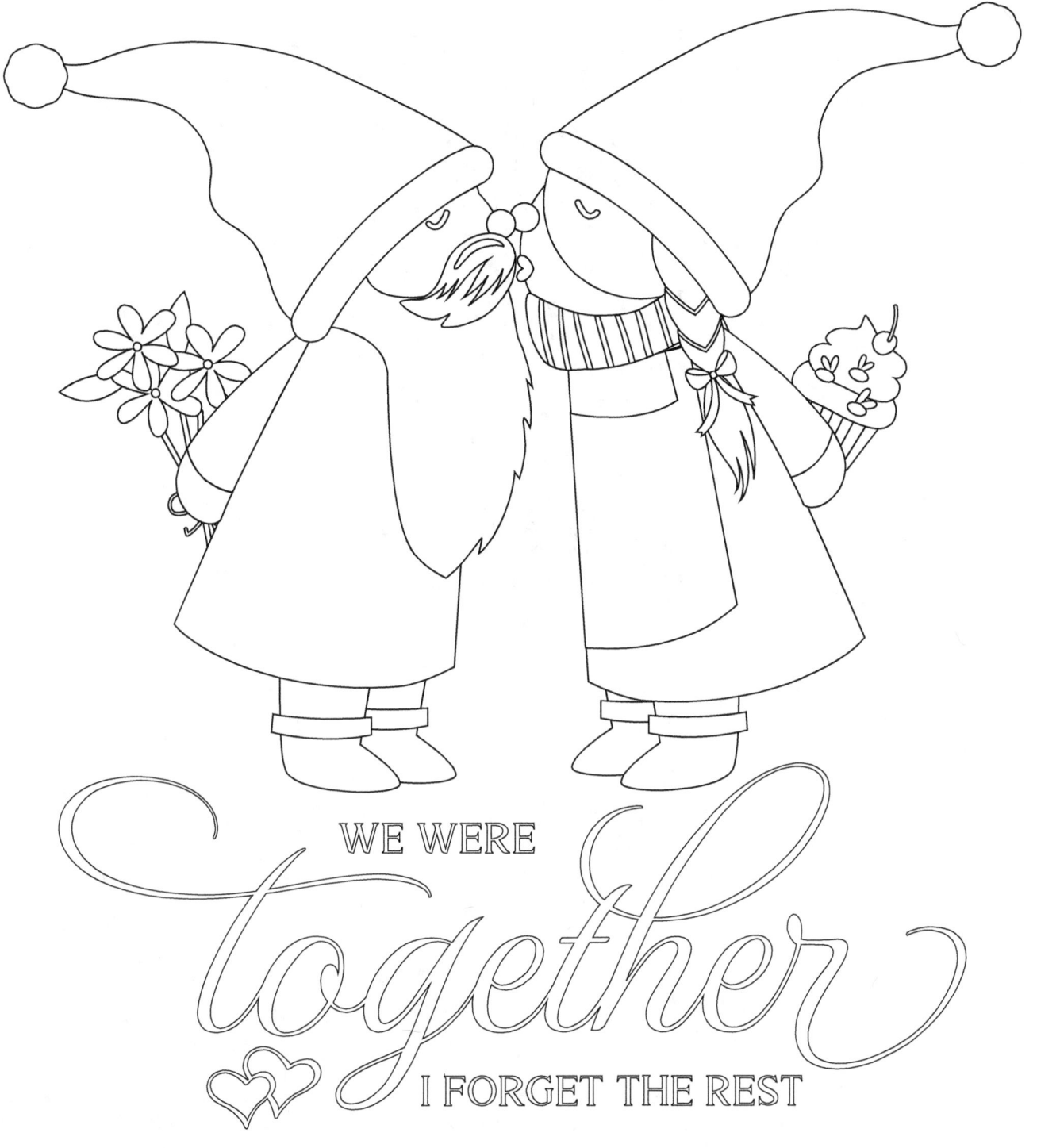

WE WERE *together* I FORGET THE REST

Colored by:	
Date completed:	
Pencils/mediums used:	

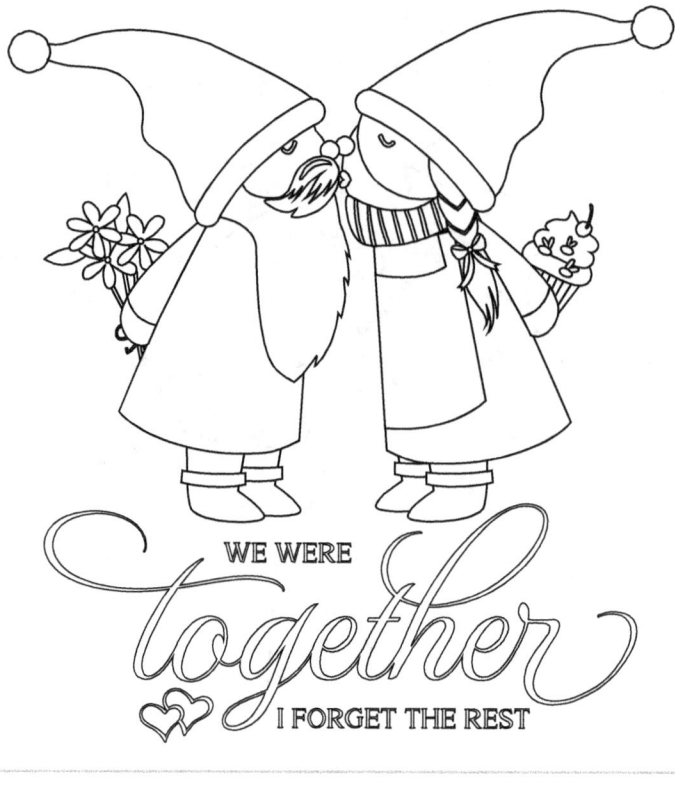

Notes and pencil & other mediums test page

Notes and pencil & other mediums test page

Thank you for purchasing this book by ChattyFred.

Visit my Amazon author page to see my other books -

amazon.com/author/chattyfred or if you are not in the US just search for ChattyFred on Amazon.

- Cute Animal Coloring Book: Sweetheart Valentines
- Mandala Coloring Dot Grid Notebook
- Mandala Adult Coloring Book
- Bunnies & Bears Sweet Valentines Notebook
- Unicorn Notebook
- And more

Like to help other people decide which books to buy?
Your opinion matters, please feel free to leave a review on Amazon

Copyright @ChattyFred 2020

www.ingramcontent.com/pod-product-compliance
Lightning Source LLC
Chambersburg PA
CBHW081100240526
45465CB00025B/2796